The Holly and The Ivy

The hol - ly and the i - vy, When they are both full grown, Of

all the trees that are in the wood, The hol - ly bears the crown.

The ris-ing of the sun And the run - ing of the deer, The

play-ing of the mer-ry or - gan, Sweet sing-ing in the choir.

The holly bears the blossom,
As white as the lily flower,
And Mary bore sweet Jesus Christ,
To be our sweet Saviour: *Refrain:*

The holly bears a berry,
As red as any blood,
And Mary bore sweet Jesus Christ,
To do poor sinners good: *Refrain:*

The holly bears a prickle,
As sharp as any thorn,
And Mary bore sweet Jesus Christ,
On Christmas Day in the morn: *Refrain:*

The holly bears a bark,
As bitter as any gall,
And Mary bore sweet Jesus Christ,
For to redeem us all: *Refrain:*

VICTORIAN CHRISTMAS
SOURCE BOOK
WITH 10 PROJECTS

Projects devised and written by Maggie Philo
Photographed by Debbie Patterson
Original Victorian Scraps from
The Archives of Mamelok Press Ltd
Created by Michelle Lovric

AURUM PRESS

VICTORIAN CHRISTMAS

Project text and design © 1995 Maggie Philo.
Text, concept and design © 1995 Michelle Lovric,
18, Monmouth Street, Covent Garden, London WC2H 9HB
Victorian Scraps © 1995 Mamelok Press Ltd.
Technical editor: Jean Kievlan.
Cover and interior design by Michelle Lovric and Lisa Pentreath.
Printed and bound in China.

Published in Great Britain and the Commonwealth by
Aurum Press Ltd, 25 Bedford Avenue, London WC1B 3AT
ISBN No:1-85410-361-X
10 9 8 7 6 5 4 3 2 1
1999 1998 1997 1996 1995

About the Victorian Scraps...

The Victorian Scraps featured in this book are from the archives of Mamelok Press Ltd. For further information about the Scraps and for details of all stockists, please write to: Mamelok Press Ltd, Northern Way, Bury St Edmunds, Suffolk IP32 6NJ, England. Telephone: 01284 762291 Facsimile: 01284 703689

About the Authors...

Maggie Philo is a highly successful designer, producing a range of beautiful interior accessories. With her extensive knowledge of specialist paint finishes, she is also in demand as a teacher and interior designer. She has been profiled in decorating magazines and exhibits regularly at important interior design shows. This is her third book about decoupage and she has also made a video about decoupage techniques and ideas. Maggie is married with five children and lives in Brighton.

Michelle Lovric runs her own company creating specialist books for major publishers. She has compiled illustrated anthologies, produced kits of books and cards, written children's stories and designed themed ranges of cards. Michelle lives and works in Covent Garden, London.

Jean Kievlan is an accomplished American craft designer and author of over ninety "how-to" craft instruction booklets and five books about crafts featuring paper scrap embellishment (published by Design Originals.) Jean is based in Fort Worth, Texas.

ACKNOWLEDGEMENTS:

The editor gratefully acknowledges the assistance of the following companies and individuals who supplied props for photography in this book:

Flower design on page 39 courtesy of Jill Peeters.

Antique toys courtesy of Veronica Shepherd at Pollock's Toy Museum, 1 Scala Street, London W1P 1LT.

Christmas garlands and decorations courtesy of William Price, Unit D, Whiteleys, Bayswater and Ealing Broadway, London.

Christmas cakes courtesy of Alberto Pagnano at Cappuccetto Patisserie, 8/9 Moor Street, London W1.

Candlesticks and Christmas decorations courtesy of Neal Street East, 5 Neal Street, London WC2H 9PU

Pictures on pages 10, 26, 37, 48 courtesy of The Fine Art Photographic Library, London.

Christmas Pudding picture on page 38 courtesy of The Mansell Collection, London.

VICTORIAN CHRISTMAS

CONTENTS

INTRODUCTION

Christmas is not a Victorian invention, but our cherished memories of the festive season are invariably traced back there. That frozen moment of time, which we try to re-create each Christmas, was probably one year exactly in the middle of the last century. Picture, as Charles Dickens did, a season of overflowing goodwill and picturesque plenty:

The tree was planted in the middle of a great round table, and towered high above their heads. It was brilliantly lighted by a multitude of little tapers; and everywhere sparkled and glittered with bright objects. There were rosy-cheeked dolls, hiding behind the green leaves; and there were real watches (with movable hands, at least, and an endless capacity of being wound up) dangling from innumerable twigs; there were French-polished tables, chairs, bedsteads, wardrobes, eight-day clocks, and various other articles of domestic furniture (wonderfully-made, in tin, at Wolverhampton), perched among the boughs, as if in preparation for some fairy house-keeping; there were jolly, broadfaced little men, much more agreeable in appearance than many real men - and no wonder, for their heads took off, and showed them to be full of sugarplums; there were fiddles and drums; there were tambourines, books, work-boxes, paint-boxes, sweetmeat-boxes, peepshow-boxes, and all kinds of boxes; there were trinkets for the elder girls, far brighter than any grown-up gold and jewels; there were baskets and pin-cushions in all devices; there were guns and swords, and banners; there were witches standing in enchanted rings of pasteboard, to tell fortunes; there were teetotums, humming-tops, needle-cases, pen-wipers, smelling-bottles, conversation-cards, bouquet-holders; real fruit, made artificially dazzling with gold leaf; imitation apples, pears, and walnuts, crammed with surprises; in short, as a pretty child, before me, delightedly whispered to another pretty child, her bosom friend, "There was everything, and more." This motley collection of odd objects, clustering on the tree like magic fruit, and flashing back the bright looks directed towards it from every side - some of the diamond-eyes admiring it were hardly on a level with the table, and a few were languishing in timid wonder on the bosoms of pretty mothers, aunts and nurses - made a lively realisation of the fancies of childhood; and set me thinking how all the trees that grow and all the things that come into existence on the earth, have their wild adornments at that well-remembered time.

But it was not ever so. When Queen Victoria came to the throne in 1837, Santa Claus, Christmas cards and Christmas stockings were all unheard of. However, for many centuries the end of the year had brought with it a tradition of celebration. Long before the birth of Christ, mankind insisted on a burst of bright merriment in the bleak midwinter. The shortest, coldest days and longest, darkest nights of the year had long been punctuated with high festivals of light and life, heralding the coming spring and the rebirth and renewal of the natural world.

The Romans had their festival of the Saturnalia, a wild and lawless celebration, when masters would become slaves and the rich would share their wealth with the poor. This was succeeded by the equally riotous Feast of Fools, governed by Lord Misrule, in medieval times. The Emperor Aurelian in the 3rd century AD had decreed that seven days in December should be set aside to worship the sun, and during the Dark Ages the twelve days of Christmas were those in which every home, however humble, burned candles to welcome even strangers to their hearth.

These ancient festivals became entangled with the celebration of the birth of Jesus Christ, which was established as December 25th by Pope Julian I during the 4th century. Despite the holiness of the occasion, the tradition of joyous and conspicuous consumption continued. The jollifications and excesses of the festivals were periodically frowned upon: the American Puritans spurned its luxury, feeling that fasting was holier than feasting, and in England the Roundheads banned the "Popish" Christmas in 1647. But with the Restoration of the British monarchy in 1660, Christmas was welcomed back with a flourish.

VICTORIAN CHRISTMAS

The Victorians adapted and re-invented many of the old customs to suit their own sentimental and aesthetic preoccupations. Victorian entrepreneurs created new festive fashions and gimmicks, such as the Christmas card, which have retained their popularity till this day. Layers of tradition and unforgettable imagery were laid in place, in much the same way that Victorians laid shawls and doilies on every surface in their homes. They fused the legends of Father Christmas and Santa Claus. They revived the ancient customs of the Yule Log, the Wassail Bowl and carolling in the night. With typical zeal, they applied the inventions of the Industrial Revolution to the arts of giving and decorating.

The Victorians made respectable "The Glorious Time of the Great Too Much," issuing a moderated licence for dizzy merriment and rich indulgence. They created a festival of happy tastes, sounds, textures and aromas: fragrant fir-trees alight with candles, vivid, prickly holly draped in garlands and flaming sticky pudding stuffed with coins. Further to delight the senses, silvery bells pealed, poignant carols were warbled and foaming toasts were offered. A few exceptionally cold winters in the early years of Victoria's reign coated all succeeding Christmases in snowy imagery, even sometimes, absurdly, in the tropical outposts of the British Empire.

The Victorian Christmas also embodied much drama and picturesque ritual: the crèche scene in every church, the nativity play; *The Nutcracker*; the Midnight Mass; the almost unbearably exciting after-dinner games, such as Snapdragon and Blind Man's Buff. Most of all the Victorians turned Christmas into the celebration of family life and values, a tradition that has happily lasted into modern times.

Christmas, after all, started with a family. Its wintry timing had made it also a festival of hearth and home. The cold outside concentrated the mind on the cosiness and comfort inside. It was, and remains, a time for travelling, as far-flung family-members gravitated homewards, for scenes of reunion, for moments of nostalgia, for affectionate remembrances of absent loved ones, for resolutions and re-dedications to the year to come.

All these things were made an official part of the Christmas iconography by the Victorians. In this book, we show how traditional Victorian imagery, in the form of Victorian "Scraps," can be used in a variety of crafts that will help re-create some of the spirit and feel of a Victorian Christmas in your own home, using your own hands and your own imagination, just as the Victorians would have done.

Victorian Scraps are small pieces of paper, printed in colour and often also embossed (stamped to produced raised surfaces) and diecut (ready-cut into shapes). The Scraps were used to decorate cards, albums, boxes and even furniture in the popular craft known as decoupage. They had first appeared at the beginning of the 19th century, and one of the first companies to provide beautiful Scraps for an ever-growing and ever more inventive public was Mamelok, which was founded in Breslau, in the late 1820s. Mamelok's Scraps are still produced today, now in England, where the company moved in 1934, and their archive of lovely Victorian Christmas designs is the basis for all the projects in this book.

The projects are arranged to cover the Christmas season chronologically, with opportunities to create Victorian-style crafts for every festive occasion - from home-made gifts and stocking fillers to Christmas crackers, a mince pie platter and a Wassail Bowl for the New Year punch.

A NOTE ABOUT MATERIALS

The following materials are used for most of the projects in this book. Additional materials specific to a particular project are listed in the relevant sections.

MANICURE SCISSORS, SMALL CRAFT KNIFE OR SCALPEL
CUTTING BOARD OR THICK CARD
P.V.A. OR WHITE CRAFT GLUE
HOUSEHOLD SPONGE
BRUSHES FOR PAINTING, GLUING AND VARNISHING
WATER-BASED SATIN ACRYLIC VARNISH

COOKIE TIN & CHRISTMAS COOKIES

Historical Perspective :
CHRISTMAS PRESENTS

Christmas was and remains a time of adornment, and therefore a time of handicrafts and invention. In early Victorian times, most people made Christmas gifts for each other. This decorated cookie jar and its home-made almond Christmas cookies could easily have been made by a Victorian lady for a friend or relative.

Toys were almost unknown except for the very rich at the beginning of Victoria's reign, but they became more accessible as the Industrial Revolution took them into mass production. Early in the century gifts were exchanged on New Year's Eve, but this was soon changed to Christmas Day.

Victorian magazines were full of ideas for presents to make - slippers, pincushions, mittens, photograph frames, penwipers. Later in the century catalogues also offered mail-order presents or people could choose gifts in the grand shops and have them delivered. This was the age of the mechanical or "wind-up" toy in the form of singing, dancing animals; also of toy trains and board games, such as snakes and ladders and tiddlywinks. Boys collected lead soldiers and girls could dream of exquisite dolls with their own extensive wardrobes. It was also the age of miniatures - perfect, small-scale theatres, circuses, forts and zoos. The hub of the doll and toymaking industry was in Germany, with some beautiful dolls also made in France, although British manufacturing began to flourish by the end of the century.

YOU WILL NEED

Round tin
Scraps from sheets 107, 54 & 55
(tall Santa figure for back of tin)
Deep red paint (emulsion, latex
or acrylic)
Metal primer (may be necessary)
Photocopies of carol music from
front endpapers of this book
Tea bag

Candle
Repositionable glue/ spray adhesive
(remountable)
Wired and unwired ribbons
Gold cord with tassels
Imitation holly
Self-stick square of adhesive or
hot melt glue gun
Fine grade sandpaper (optional)

CHRISTMAS PRESENTS continued...

The giving of presents involved a breathless round of shopping, making, wrapping, all imbued with the extra glamour of secrecy. The complicated recipes of the period provided endless opportunities for shopping in the frosty, festive high streets. Charles Dickens described the scene beautifully:

The Grocers'! oh the Grocers'! nearly closed, with perhaps two shutters down, or one: but through those gaps such glimpses! It was not alone that the scales descending on the counter made a merry sound, or that the twine and roller parted company so briskly, or that the canisters were rattled up and down like juggling tricks, or even that the blended scents of the tea and coffee were so grateful to the nose, or even that the raisins were so plentiful and rare, the almonds so extremely white, the sticks of cinnamon so long and straight, the other spices so delicious, the candied fruits so caked and spotted with molten sugar as to make the coldest looker-on feel faint and subsequently bilious. Nor was it that the figs were moist and pulpy, or that the French plums blushed in modest tartness from their highly-decorated boxes, or that everything was good to eat and in its Christmas dress; but the hopeful customers were all so hurried and so eager in the hopeful promise of the day, that they tumbled up against each other at the door, crashing their wicker baskets wildly, and left their purchases upon the counter, and came running back to fetch them, and committed hundreds of little mistakes, in the best humour possible...

RECIPE FOR CHRISTMAS COOKIES

12 oz (350g) ground almonds
2 large egg whites
5 oz (150g) caster sugar
2 teaspoons (2 x 5ml) cinnamon
1/4 teaspoon (1.25ml) almond extract
Icing sugar for dusting
Butter for greasing

Beat the egg whites until fairly stiff then gradually add the caster sugar. Beat until the mixture becomes very stiff then set aside four heaped tablespoonfuls. Add the almonds, cinnamon and extract to the remaining mixture and knead it until it is well blended. Dust icing sugar onto a flat surface and roll the dough out to a thickness of about 1/4 inch (1/2 cm). Cut out the dough using Christmas shaped cookie cutters and place them on a greased baking sheet. Brush the top of each cookie with the remaining egg white mix and cook for about 20 minutes in the oven at a temperature of l50 degrees C (300 F), gas mark 2.

COOKIE TIN
STEP BY STEP

1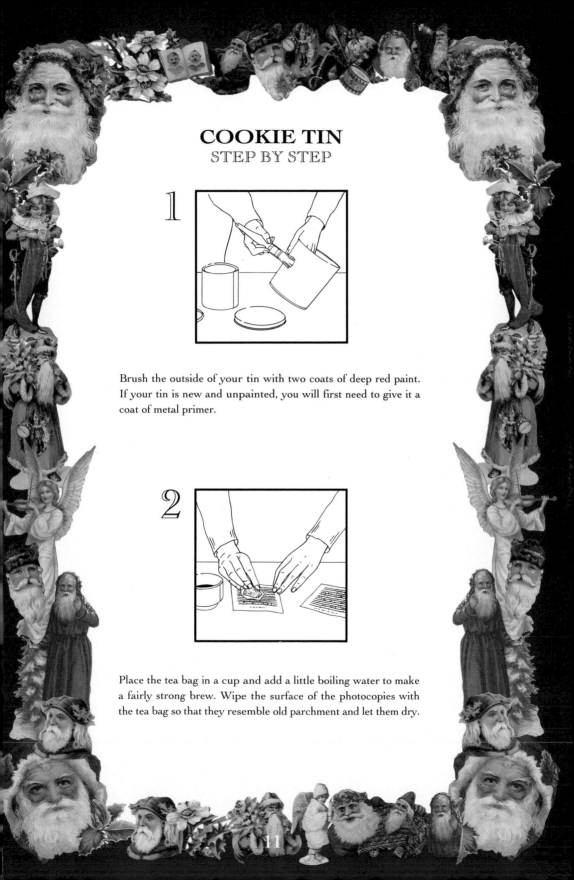

Brush the outside of your tin with two coats of deep red paint.
If your tin is new and unpainted, you will first need to give it a
coat of metal primer.

2

Place the tea bag in a cup and add a little boiling water to make
a fairly strong brew. Wipe the surface of the photocopies with
the tea bag so that they resemble old parchment and let them dry.

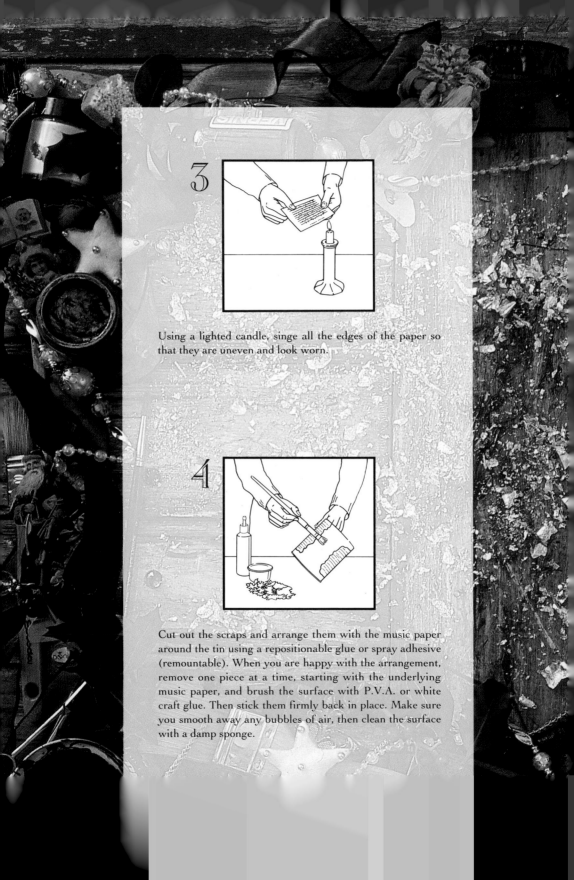

3

Using a lighted candle, singe all the edges of the paper so that they are uneven and look worn.

4

Cut out the scraps and arrange them with the music paper around the tin using a repositionable glue or spray adhesive (remountable). When you are happy with the arrangement, remove one piece at a time, starting with the underlying music paper, and brush the surface with P.V.A. or white craft glue. Then stick them firmly back in place. Make sure you smooth away any bubbles of air, then clean the surface with a damp sponge.

5

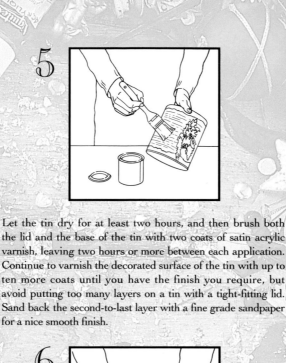

Let the tin dry for at least two hours, and then brush both the lid and the base of the tin with two coats of satin acrylic varnish, leaving two hours or more between each application. Continue to varnish the decorated surface of the tin with up to ten more coats until you have the finish you require, but avoid putting too many layers on a tin with a tight-fitting lid. Sand back the second-to-last layer with a fine grade sandpaper for a nice smooth finish.

6

Tie a bow with wired ribbon, place the end of the piece of holly through the centre and attach this to the lid with a self-stick adhesive pad or hot melt glue gun. When in position, tie a second bow of contrasting ribbon around this. Finally, add a cord with a tassel at each end to the rim of the lid. If you cannot find one ready-made, make your own by adding tassels to the ends of a piece of cord with gold thread.

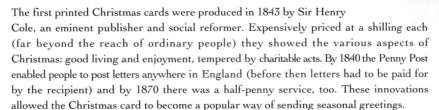

POT POURRI HOLDER & GIFT TAG

Historical Perspective: CHRISTMAS CARDS

The first printed Christmas cards were produced in 1843 by Sir Henry Cole, an eminent publisher and social reformer. Expensively priced at a shilling each (far beyond the reach of ordinary people) they showed the various aspects of Christmas: good living and enjoyment, tempered by charitable acts. By 1840 the Penny Post enabled people to post letters anywhere in England (before then letters had to be paid for by the recipient) and by 1870 there was a half-penny service, too. These innovations allowed the Christmas card to become a popular way of sending seasonal greetings.

The forerunners of these cards were the "Christmas Pieces" which school children were required to complete at the end of their winter term each year. These pieces were to show off their calligraphic and artistic skills for the benefit of their proud parents. The printed card was a natural extension of this idea.

Printing technology was enhanced during the period and the costs came down sufficiently to allow the printing of the cards to fit most pockets. The success of the Christmas card industry led to the incorporation of all kinds of new ideas - embossing, foiling, gilding and many other innovations. The "pop-up" three-dimensional card was a Victorian invention, as was the "diecut" or shaped card. Paper engineering became extravagantly creative - there were fan-cards and rocking cards and cards trimmed with satin, silk and brocade. Paper was punched out into details as intricate as lace. Glitter was sprinkled and glued. Sentimental messages and poems were often added in elaborate typography.

In Victorian times, Christmas cards did not invariably show Christmas images. Flowers, landscapes, jokes, and stories were popular. Mamelok's archives include chickens, eggs, comic scenes, gothic calligraphy and many other un-Christmaslike pictures. However, Santa, angels, bells, church scenes and trees certainly played their part.

Two Christmas cards from the Mamelok Collection.

Many people made their own cards, often using the beautiful embossed cut-outs or Scraps manufactured by companies like Mamelok. The Scraps were used as the central illustration and surrounded with paper doilies, ribbons, feathers, shells or lace.

This project, a pot pourri holder with its own gift tag, is one which might well have been made as a Christmas gift during Victorian times, demonstrating the Victorian love of embellishment and fine handwork, and including the much-loved cherub imagery of the period. The open-worked lid is designed to allow the fragrance of the pot pourri to escape.

YOU WILL NEED

Wide-necked glass vase approx
 3.75" (9.5 cm) in diameter at top
Scraps from sheet 60
Gold doily
Small circle of gold card or a piece
 of brass foil 4"(10cm) long cut to the
 same diameter as the neck of the vase.
Gold card approx 3"x 2" (7.5 x 5 cm)
Burgundy card approx 2.75"x 1.75"
 (7 x 4.5 cm)
Gold fine-tip marking pen
Ruler
Metallic gold cord
2 metallic gold tassels
Burgundy wired ribbon 15" (38cm)

RECIPE FOR POT POURRI

You can make your own Christmas pot pourri by putting together the following ingredients and adding essential oils of rose, orange, cinnamon and cloves.

Dried orange peel, pine cones, bay leaves, dried rose petals, cinnamon sticks, allspice berries, cloves, aniseed.

Mix the ingredients together, add the fragrant oils a drop at a time and stir well. Store the pot pourri in a container (not metal) with a tight-fitting lid for between two and four weeks before turning it out into the glass bowl.

POT POURRI HOLDER
STEP BY STEP

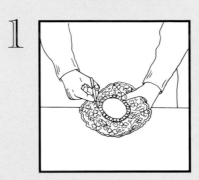

1

To make the lid, cut out the middle of a gold doily and stick it on the underside of a piece of gold card. Use a craft knife to trim away excess card. If you cannot find an appropriate doily to fit the size of the mouth of your jar, use the gold card on its own, cut to size. (Alternatively, you could use a piece of brass foil, cut out to the shape of the lid. Put the foil circle face down on a folded newspaper and draw a design of stars, curving lines etc on the back, using a ballpoint pen with the ink removed, pressing very hard to make the design appear, as if embossed, on the front of the foil.)

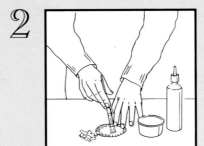

2

Cut out the cherub scraps. Brush the surface of the lid with P.V.A. or white craft glue and press the biggest scrap firmly in position in the middle of the lid. Clean off the excess glue with a damp sponge.

3

When the lid is thoroughly dry, cut away the excess card, using a sharp craft knife, so that you are left with a half inch rim around the edge of the lid (to which the head and feet of the cherub are attached) so that a thin gold edge remains around the figure.

4

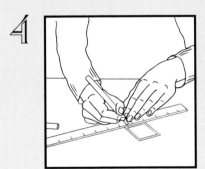

To make the gift tag, glue the burgundy card on top of the gold card and, using a fine gold marker pen and ruler, draw a gold border just inside the burgundy card. Make a small hole in one corner of the tag with a paper punch and then thread the cord through. Attach tassels to the ends by winding them together with gold thread. Finally, tie a piece of burgundy wired ribbon around the vase and attach the gift tag. (Optional - you may prefer to keep the vase simple, so that the pot pourri can be seen clearly through the glass. But if you want a thoroughly decorated gift, you can add an extra doily "collar").

CHRISTMAS CANDLE

Historical Perspective :
DECORATING THE HOUSE

The focal point of Christmas, the tree, was traditionally put up the night before Christmas, but the decorating of the house began weeks earlier, with mistletoe, holly, ivy and evergreen garlanding every available surface. This tradition originated in ancient times, when it was thought that a holly tree planted near the house would prevent it from being struck by lightning. The idea was expanded in Scandinavia, where green branches were thought to ward off evil. Moreover, bringing bright boughs of holly into the home in midwinter betokened spring and the return of greenness and new life. The medieval druids thought that the sun took refuge in the sacred holly tree during the winter, while the Christian interpretation was that holly prickles recalled Christ's crown of thorns, and the red berries the drops of blood that fell from his wounds. The Victorians delighted in this picturesque custom and the collecting, buying and festooning of the holly garlands was a well-loved part of their Christmas ritual. The American custom of hanging a wreath on the front door was welcomed into Victorian England.

Here is Charles Dickens again:

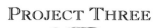

The walls and ceilings were so hung with living green, that it looked a perfect grove; from every part of which, bright gleaming berries glistened. The crisp leaves of holly, mistletoe, and ivy reflected back the light, as if so many little mirrors had been scattered there ...

Another important piece of greenery was the mistletoe bough, under which everyone was supposed to kiss. Indeed, before the advent of the tree, it was the focal point of the decoration.

Christmas was a celebration of home and the Victorians adored its vivid clutter. Everything was cleaned and polished, the finest linen, silver and the best China tea service were all brought out.

The cold outside emphasised the warmth inside, candles and oil lamps casting their mellow glow. This simple project is again one which might have been created in a real Victorian home, in the exciting weeks before Christmas.

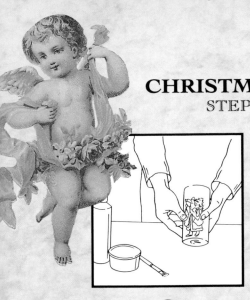

CHRISTMAS CANDLE
STEP BY STEP

1

Cut out the scraps and brush the backs with P.V.A. or white craft glue. Stick them firmly in place towards the lower end of the candle so that Father Christmas does not get burnt!

2

Wrap the gold cake banding around the base and glue together at the back. Use a strip of gold foil paper if you cannot find cake banding.

3

Glue on the stars around the top. You could use paper stars or hand paint them on if you prefer. In the interests of safety, you should not let your candle burn to the level of the paper. You could place a night light inside the candle once it has melted down sufficiently and so extend its life.

YOU WILL NEED

Large red candle
Scraps from sheets 58 and 55 (short Santa figure for the reverse side)
Gold foil cake banding
Gold metallic stars
Plaid ribbon

CHRISTMAS TREE BUCKET

Historical Perspective:
CHRISTMAS TREES

The idea of a Christmas tree came from Germany and the German-born English King George III is known to have installed one in his palace. His granddaughter Queen Victoria ensured its popularity in England when she and her German husband Prince Albert had a Christmas tree at Windsor Castle in 1849. The royal family was depicted with their tree in the *Illustrated London News* in 1848. The Christmas tree appeared in America at around the same time, probably introduced by German settlers in Pennsylvania.

Originally, Christmas trees were decorated with fruit and nuts and small gifts. They were often set up on a central table in the main reception room. This project, a Christmas Tree Bucket, has been created using the traditional Victorian craft of decoupage, in which a prepared surface is decorated with Scraps which are then coated with many layers of varnish so that the edges of the cut-outs disappear and the finished piece looks as if it has been hand-painted with the images.

YOU WILL NEED

Metal bucket
Scraps from sheets 53, 57, 58, 97 & 108.
  (51, 67, 68 & 100 on reverse)
Metal primer
Dark green paint (emulsion, latex or acrylic)
Metallic gold paint
Repositionable glue or spray adhesive (remountable)
Fine grade sandpaper

CHRISTMAS TREE BUCKET
STEP BY STEP

1

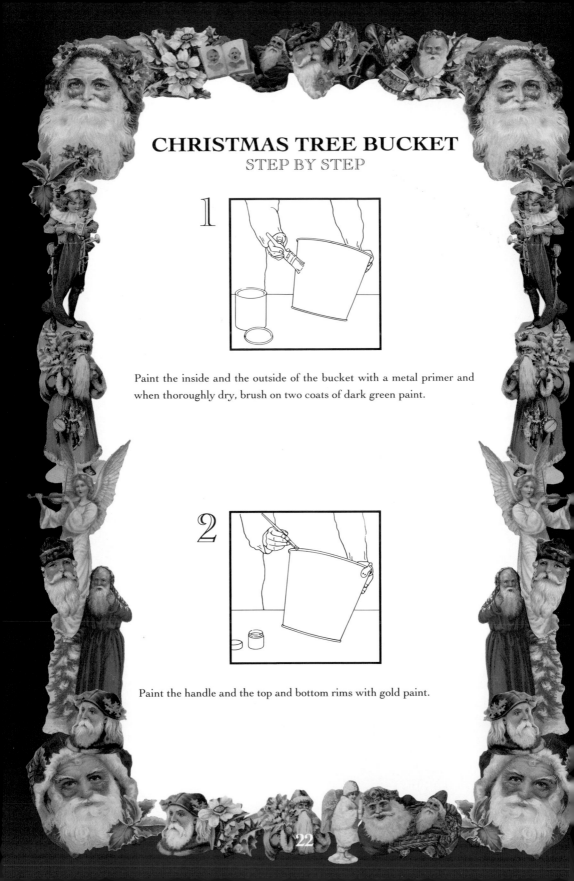

Paint the inside and the outside of the bucket with a metal primer and when thoroughly dry, brush on two coats of dark green paint.

2

Paint the handle and the top and bottom rims with gold paint.

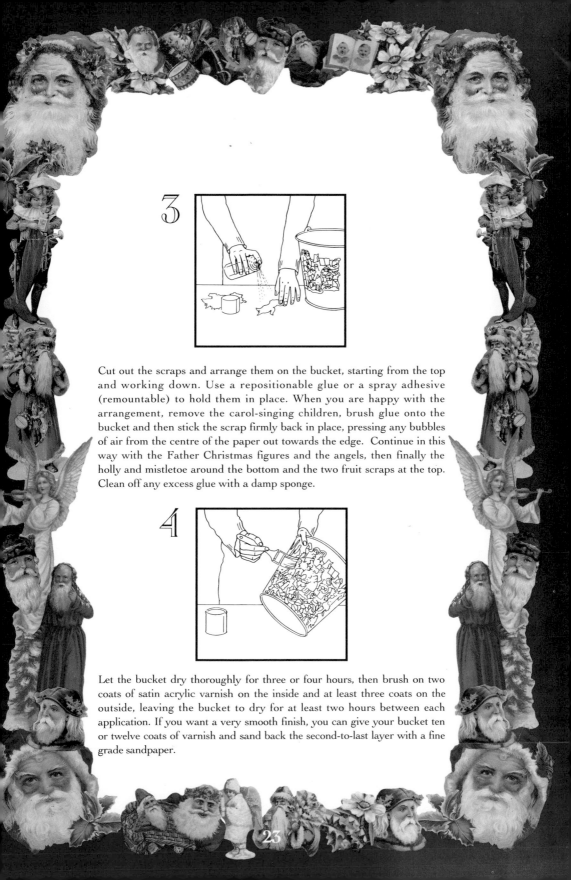

3

Cut out the scraps and arrange them on the bucket, starting from the top
and working down. Use a repositionable glue or a spray adhesive
(remountable) to hold them in place. When you are happy with the
arrangement, remove the carol-singing children, brush glue onto the
bucket and then stick the scrap firmly back in place, pressing any bubbles
of air from the centre of the paper out towards the edge. Continue in this
way with the Father Christmas figures and the angels, then finally the
holly and mistletoe around the bottom and the two fruit scraps at the top.
Clean off any excess glue with a damp sponge.

4

Let the bucket dry thoroughly for three or four hours, then brush on two
coats of satin acrylic varnish on the inside and at least three coats on the
outside, leaving the bucket to dry for at least two hours between each
application. If you want a very smooth finish, you can give your bucket ten
or twelve coats of varnish and sand back the second-to-last layer with a fine
grade sandpaper.

CHRISTMAS DECORATIONS

The decoration of Victorian Christmas trees became increasingly elaborate. Fruit and nuts at the beginning of the century were later supplemented with toys and confectionery. The tree would be laden with candles, which were lit on Christmas Eve and New Year's Eve. The star at its top recalled the Biblical star. People often made their own decorations, with children using a glue made of flour and water. Popular images were bells, stars and Santas. By the late 1800s glass ornaments, gilded and foiled paper and three dimensional ornaments were being manufactured. Angels were particularly popular. Glass balls and fabric ornaments were imported from Germany and Holland.

These same glass balls are still popular, and this project shows how to embellish them with 19th century images to create tree decorations with an authentic Victorian feel.

CHRISTMAS DECORATIONS
STEP BY STEP

1 Carefully cut out all the scraps. For the balls with the pretty flower borders, start by brushing the back of a border with glue and sticking it around one of the baubles vertically. Do the same with the remaining two. Next glue scraps onto both sides of all six balls.

2 Glue some cord or braid around the three balls without the paper border. Clean off all excess glue before it dries. Finally, add a pretty ribbon or gold cord to the top of each ball to attach it to the tree.

You Will Need

Six plain glass Christmas balls large enough
  to take the scraps
Small Scraps from sheets 54, 55, 56, 57,
  59, 60, 68, & 97. Borders from sheet 99
Metallic gold cord or narrow braid
Ribbons

Historical Perspective :
CHRISTMAS EVE TRADITIONS

On Christmas Eve everyone who could do so would be travelling to the family home. The celebration of the holy family had become a celebration of all family life, with everyone coming from far and wide to be with their loved ones in the festive season. Washington Irving, an American writer who toured Victorian England to record the Christmas celebrations, observed:

I rode for a long distance in one of the public coaches, on the day preceding Christmas. The coach was crowded, both inside and out, with passengers, who, by their talk, seemed principally bound to the mansions of relations or friends to eat the Christmas Dinner. It was loaded also with hampers of game, and baskets and boxes of delicacies: and hares hung dangling their long ears about the coachman's box...

With the family finally assembled, Christmas Eve was the time for all the traditional Christmas games, such as Snapdragon. In this dangerously exciting game, brandy was poured over a bowl of currants and then set alight. The players took turns to snatch the burning hot currants from the flames and put them into their mouths.

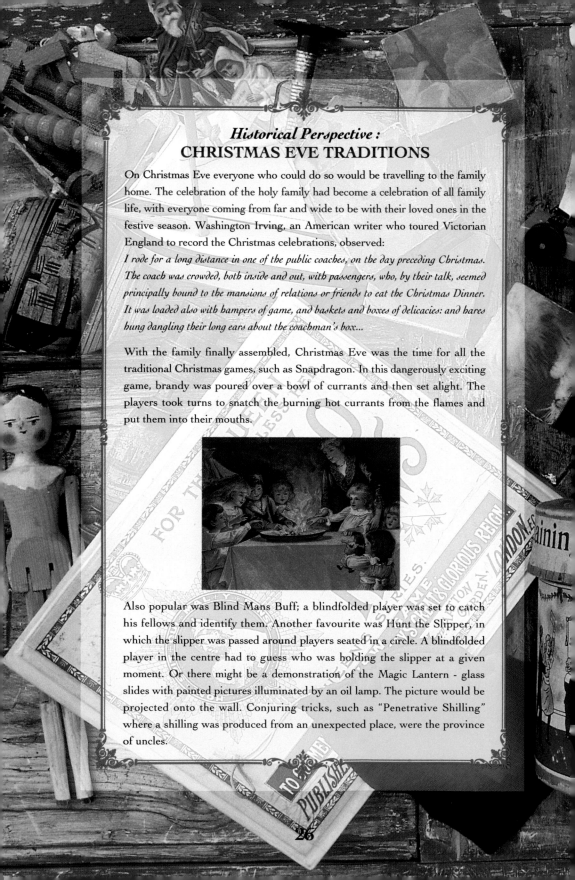

Also popular was Blind Mans Buff; a blindfolded player was set to catch his fellows and identify them. Another favourite was Hunt the Slipper, in which the slipper was passed around players seated in a circle. A blindfolded player in the centre had to guess who was holding the slipper at a given moment. Or there might be a demonstration of the Magic Lantern - glass slides with painted pictures illuminated by an oil lamp. The picture would be projected onto the wall. Conjuring tricks, such as "Penetrative Shilling" where a shilling was produced from an unexpected place, were the province of uncles.

Everyone could join in the singing of the Christmas songs, the dancing, and the guessing game of charades, which originated in recitations of poetry or performances on musical instruments given by the younger members of the family. Charaders would mime words, phrases or titles, and everyone would have to guess what they were portraying. Even more elaborate were the home-produced plays and spectacles enacted in the more affluent families.

In Victorian times, Midnight Mass on Christmas Eve was a well-loved tradition. Churches would have been decorated with holly and ivy, and nativity scenes lovingly created by the parishioners. The idea of a crèche scene seems to have originated in Italy in the 13th century. St Francis of Assisi unveiled one to the peasants of his parish, to their lasting delight. The custom became more elaborate as it crossed the Alps and spread throughout Europe.

The streets outside the churches resounded with carols - the Victorians revived the medieval custom of Christmas songs. The carol "O Come, All Ye Faithful" was translated from Latin in 1843. In 1868 "Little Town of Bethlehem" was published. "Away in a Manger" emerged in the USA in 1883. Other carols were added to the repertoire or revived from old classics as the century progressed.

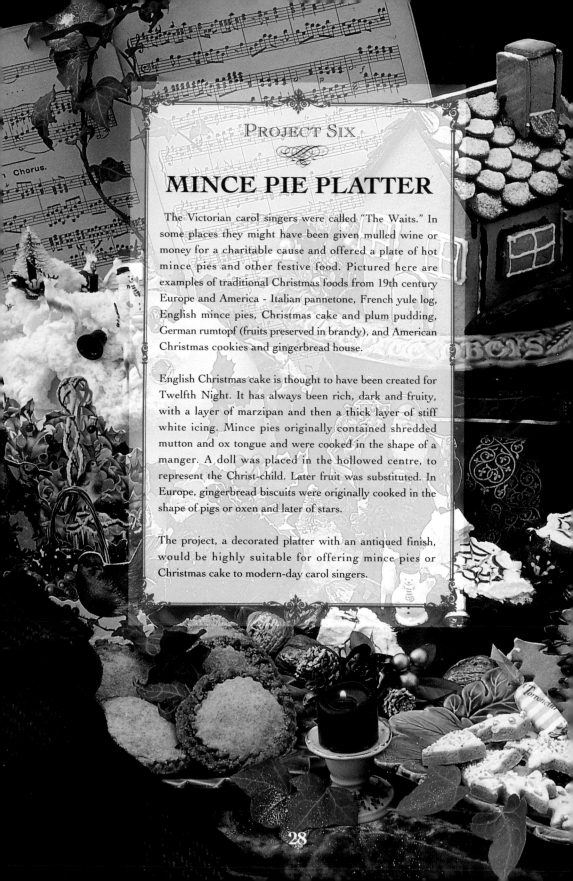

MINCE PIE PLATTER

The Victorian carol singers were called "The Waits." In some places they might have been given mulled wine or money for a charitable cause and offered a plate of hot mince pies and other festive food. Pictured here are examples of traditional Christmas foods from 19th century Europe and America - Italian pannetone, French yule log, English mince pies, Christmas cake and plum pudding, German rumtopf (fruits preserved in brandy), and American Christmas cookies and gingerbread house.

English Christmas cake is thought to have been created for Twelfth Night. It has always been rich, dark and fruity, with a layer of marzipan and then a thick layer of stiff white icing. Mince pies originally contained shredded mutton and ox tongue and were cooked in the shape of a manger. A doll was placed in the hollowed centre, to represent the Christ-child. Later fruit was substituted. In Europe, gingerbread biscuits were originally cooked in the shape of pigs or oxen and later of stars.

The project, a decorated platter with an antiqued finish, would be highly suitable for offering mince pies or Christmas cake to modern-day carol singers.

YOU WILL NEED

Glass plate (this one has a gold border)

Scraps from sheets 51, 57 & 67

Gold doily

Ageing varnish or a yellowing
   polyurethane varnish

Dark green paint (emulsion, latex or acrylic)

MINCE PIE PLATTER
STEP BY STEP

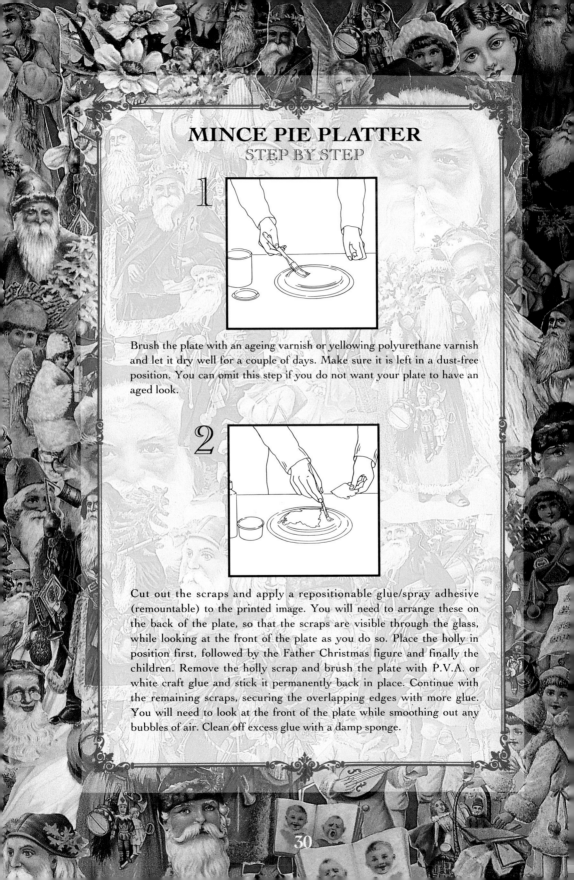

1 Brush the plate with an ageing varnish or yellowing polyurethane varnish and let it dry well for a couple of days. Make sure it is left in a dust-free position. You can omit this step if you do not want your plate to have an aged look.

2 Cut out the scraps and apply a repositionable glue/spray adhesive (remountable) to the printed image. You will need to arrange these on the back of the plate, so that the scraps are visible through the glass, while looking at the front of the plate as you do so. Place the holly in position first, followed by the Father Christmas figure and finally the children. Remove the holly scrap and brush the plate with P.V.A. or white craft glue and stick it permanently back in place. Continue with the remaining scraps, securing the overlapping edges with more glue. You will need to look at the front of the plate while smoothing out any bubbles of air. Clean off excess glue with a damp sponge.

3

If your doily does not lie flat on the back of the plate, make a series of little cuts, half an inch (1cm) apart, all the way round. This allows it to overlap a little where you have made the cut so that it will fit the shape of your plate. Brush the plate with glue and stick the doily in place. You will need to press very firmly and look at the front of the plate while smoothing away bubbles of air. Particular care needs to be taken to eliminate air bubbles when working with glass as they can show when the glue is dry. Once again, clean the excess glue off the plate with a damp sponge.

4

Leave the plate overnight to let the glue dry thoroughly, then seal the back of the plate with a layer of acrylic varnish to prevent the possibility of paint creeping under the edges of the paper. If varnish seeps under the paper, make sure this has dried out before moving on to the next step.

MINCE PIE PLATTER
STEP BY STEP

5

Paint the back of the plate with two coats of dark green paint.

6

Seal the back of the plate with three coats of acrylic varnish, leaving two hours between each layer. After a few days you will be able to wash your plate carefully by hand, but do not put it in the dishwasher.

RECIPE FOR MINCE PIES

FOR THE PASTRY:
12oz (350g) plain flour (white or wholemeal)
3oz (75g) lard or white vegetable shortening
3oz (75g) butter or margarine   Cold water to mix

FOR THE FILLING:
1 lb (450g) cooking apples   2 oz (50g) almonds chopped or sliced
1 lb (450g) shredded suet   6 oz (175g) chopped mixed peel
1 lb (450g) currants   Grated rind and juice of 2 large lemons
1 lb (450g) raisins   2 teaspoons (10ml) ground mixed spice
1 lb (450g) brown sugar   6 tablespoons (90ml) brandy
8 oz (225g) sultanas or golden raisins

Mix all the filling ingredients together and put in clean dry jars. Keep for three to four weeks before using. For this amount of pastry, you will need about 1.5 lbs (675g) of mincemeat. The rest can be stored for next Christmas.

FOR THE TOP:
Milk and sugar

Pre-heat the oven to 200 degrees C(400F), gas mark 6. Make the pastry and put it in the refrigerator for half an hour, then roll it out fairly thinly. Cut out rounds of pastry to the size to line your patty tins and some smaller rounds to cover the pies. Grease the patty tins and line with pastry. Fill with mincemeat up to the level of the pastry, and cover with the pastry lids. Pinch or crimp the edges of the pastry together. Brush the top with milk and sprinkle with sugar. Make a small cut in the middle of each one with a knife and cook in the oven for about twenty-five minutes until nicely browned.

Historical Perspective:
CHRISTMAS PRESENTS

From the 1870s stockings were hung up on Christmas Eve in England, though in other countries, a pair of slippers was used. Rich children found them filled with toys - the poor might find a penny or an apple or an orange. Few children were denied the joy of a night-time visit from Father Christmas, or Santa Claus, with his bulging sack of gifts. It is thought that the stocking tradition originated with St Nicholas, bishop of Myra in Turkey in the 4th century. He took pity on three poor dowryless girls and tossed bags of gold through their window. The gold landed in their stockings, which had been hung up in the fireplace to dry.

The Victorian Santa Claus is a composite figure with both pagan and Christian forebears. He is partly St Nicholas, or Sinter Klaas, as he was called in Holland. Dutch settlers in America took Sinter Klaas with them and from 1870 the stories travelled back to England with the new name Santa Claus. He had a reindeer, a sleigh and toys for the children and he became mixed with the Father Christmas of English tradition, who was part of the old midwinter festivals. Whether St Nick or Sinta Klaas, he was the jovial embodiment of the spirit of Christmas.

It is thought that the idea of Santa Claus entering homes via the chimney originated in Lapland, where the igloos had only one hole in the roof for both a chimney and a door. Santa's classic appearance was shaped by Clement Moore's well-loved poem, "The Night Before Christmas," which was first published in the United States in 1823.

He was dressed all in fur from his head to his foot
And his clothes were all tarnished with ashes and soot;
A bundle of toys he had flung on his back,
And he looked like a peddler just opening his pack.
His eyes, how they twinkled! his dimples, how merry!
His cheeks were like roses, his nose like a cherry;
His droll little mouth was drawn up like a bow,
And the beard on his chin was as white as the snow...
He had a broad face, and a little round belly
That shook, when he laughed, like a bowl full of jelly,
He was chubby and plump - a right jolly old elf -
And I laughed when I saw him, in spite of myself.

CANDY BOX WITH HOME-MADE SWEETS

The ingredients for a Victorian stocking varied according to the times and the wealth of the family, but chocolate money, an orange, and an old penny were frequently included, together with home-made sweets like these peppermint creams.

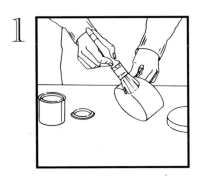

1

Paint the lid and the base of the box with two coats of dark blue paint.

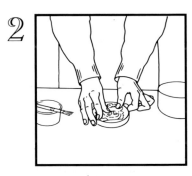

2

Brush the lid of the box with glue and press the scrap firmly into position. Clean off any excess glue with a damp sponge and let the box dry.

3

Varnish the lid and the base of the box with three coats of satin acrylic varnish, leaving two hours drying time between each one.

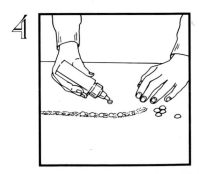

4

Glue the gemstones onto the lace or braid and let them dry before gluing the fabric around the box. Glue on the ric rac and finally tie the ribbon around the box.

RECIPE FOR PEPPERMINT CREAMS

1 large egg white   1 - 2 teaspoons (5-10ml) peppermint extract

12 oz (350g) sifted icing sugar   Green and red food colouring (optional)

Whisk the egg white until it is fluffy, then gradually add the sifted icing sugar. Add the peppermint extract to taste and knead the mixture in the bowl, adding a little additional icing sugar if necessary to form a stiff dough. Roll out the mixture, half at a time, between two sheets of non-stick baking parchment or waxed paper to a thickness of about 1/4 inch (6 mm) and stamp out 1 inch (2.5 cm) rounds. Do the same with the remaining mix. If you have some holly leaf cutters, you could cut out a few leaves as well. Roll a little piece of dough in the palm of your hand to make the berries. Leave the peppermint creams to dry for twenty-four hours. Paint the leaves and berries with the food colouring if you wish.

Historical Perspective :
CHRISTMAS DAY, CHRISTMAS CRACKERS
CHRISTMAS DINNER

In England and in America, Christmas Day was the pinnacle of all delights but in continental Europe presents were exchanged on St Nicholas's Day (December 6th), on Christmas Eve or at Epiphany on January 6th, the day when the Three Wise Men beheld the infant Christ and presented their gifts of myrrh, frankincense and gold.

The classic Christmas Day began at dawn with the joyful discovery and feverish dismembering of the bulging stocking at the end of the bed. Bigger presents were opened under the tree either later in the morning, after church or after the midday meal.

The church bells tolled out for Christmas Day and the morning's service whetted the appetite for the ritually enormous Christmas dinner. At the table the family would find decorations, like the centrepiece and Christmas crackers shown overleaf.

Christmas crackers were table decorations which popped open to reveal a gift - invented by a London confectioner, Tom Smith, in 1846. The idea was adapted from French bonbons, candies wrapped in a twist of coloured paper.

Tom Smith embellished his bonbons by borrowing from the Chinese tradition of putting paper mottoes inside, like fortune cookies, and he adapted the techniques of Chinese firecrackers to make them pop loudly as they were opened. They were a great success and even more so when he added paper hats and small toys. The crackers in this project are trimmed with ribbons and patterned papers, including tartan, which became very popular during the Victorian period. Queen Victoria showed a great fondness for all things Scottish and spent many happy holidays at her castle at Balmoral in the Scottish highlands. A popular decoration for Christmas crackers used to be silhouettes - the profiles of well-known political characters.

After pulling their Christmas crackers, and donning their paper crowns, the Victorians settled down to the serious business of eating. Turkey was not compulsory. In the North of England people favoured roast beef while goose was preferred in the South and also in Germany. Queen Victoria ate roast swan with her family on Christmas Day in 1840. Boar's head was another object of culinary desire. Turkeys were eaten by the Aztecs, enjoyed by the early American settlers and brought to Britain in the 16th century. Henry VIII is thought to have been the first British monarch to eat a turkey.

Pip in Charles Dickens' novel *Great Expectations* dined on roast pork and fowls, while in *A Christmas Carol* a goose was comsumed by the Cratchit family on Christmas morning. The goose was gradually overtaken by the turkey as the classic Christmas Day dish. Whatever the meat, it would be accompanied by Brussels sprouts, turnips, potatoes, bread sauce, cranberry or apple sauce, and a stuffing of herbs, onions and breadcrumbs. In Scandinavia, the pig-slaughtering season coincided with Christmas, and the sacrifice of the pig became part of the Christmas ritual. Roast pork was customary all over Europe from medieval times, and indeed the boar's head, with an apple between its teeth, and decorated with rosemary, was often a centrepiece. Roast peacock was another popular dish among the wealthy, and its flesh would sometimes be gilded.

TABLE CENTREPIECE & CHRISTMAS CRACKERS

In Victorian England, the climax of the meal was always the Christmas pudding, boiled for hours in a copper washing cauldron, perfectly round, full of sixpences, holly-topped and alight with blue brandy flames, as captured by Dickens in *A Christmas Carol*:

Hallo! A great deal of steam! The pudding was out of the copper. A smell like a washing-day! That was the cloth. A smell like an eating-house and pastrycook's next door to each other, with a laundress's next door to that! That was the pudding! In half a minute Mrs Cratchit entered - flushed, but smiling proudly - with the pudding, like a speckled cannon-ball, so hard and firm, blazing in half of half-a-quarter of ignited brandy, and bedight with Christmas holly stuck into the top.

The preparation of this pudding had started many weeks earlier. While it was being made each member of the family would be required to stir it once, at the same time making a wish. Then silver coins and brandy were added. It had to be stirred from East to West, in the spirit of the Three Wise Men.

YOU WILL NEED

CRACKERS
Scraps from sheets 54, 58, 60, 68 & 100
Glue stick
Card tube measuring 16 inches and 2 inches (40 and 5 cm) in diameter (optional)
20 inch (50 cm) length of twine.

AND FOR EACH CRACKER:
Foil paper 15 x 7.75 inches (37.5 x 19.5 cm)
Thin card - 1 piece 7 x 5 inches (17.5 x 12.5 cm), 2 pieces 7 x 2.5 inches (17.5 x 6.25 cm)

Thin white paper for lining 7.5 x 14.5 inches (18.75 x 36.25 cm)
2 x 7.25 inch (5 x 18 cm) lengths of decorative paper or ribbon borders
2 lengths of pretty wired or unwired ribbon, cord or lace for tying around waist.

Optional : a snap (two thin strips of card with a small cracker where they join - available in craft shops or in Christmas cracker kits available by mail order from Christmas supply companies)
Motto and small gift

You Will Need

CENTREPIECE

Flower pot 4.5 – 5 inches
(11.5 – 12.6cm) high
Scrap from sheet 55
Red, dark green, light green and gold paint
Oasis ball 5 – 6 inches (12.6 – 15 cm) in diameter
One length of gold cord measuring
approximately 15 inches (38 cm)

One length of gold cord measuring
approximately 30 inches (76 cm)
Two gold tassels
60 – 70 heads of dried red roses with 1 -2
inch (2.5 – 5 cm) stems
Dark green reindeer moss
Hot melt glue gun
Pencil
Artificial holly

CENTREPIECE
STEP BY STEP

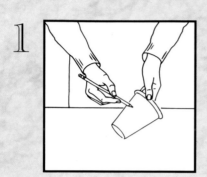

1

Paint the flower pot with two coats of dark green paint. When this has dried, draw lines lightly on the surface where you want to have your red stripes, leaving space between for narrower light green and gold stripes.

Paint the red stripes on the flower pot and let it dry. Again, lightly draw lines for guidance and paint on the narrow green stripes using a fine brush. When these are dry, paint the gold stripes, so that you achieve a "plaid" effect.

2

3

Brush some glue onto the flower pot and stick the scrap in place, smoothing away any bubbles of air from the middle of the paper towards the edge. Clean off the excess glue with a damp sponge and let it dry. Apply three coats of varnish to the pot, leaving two hours between each coat.

4

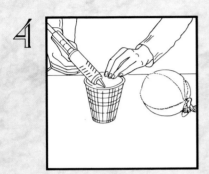

Attach tassels to both ends of the longer length of cord, using gold thread to bind them together. Divide the ball into four segments by using the end of a pencil to score the surface lightly, defining their position. Loosely tie both lengths of cord around the ball over the marks you have made. Using a hot melt glue gun, apply glue to the inside rim of the flower pot. Place the oasis ball in position inside the pot.

Untie the cords at the top and cover all four score marks with strips of moss, using the hot melt glue gun to stick them in place. Alternatively, make little wire pegs by bending two inch lengths of florists' wire into a U-shape and use these to attach the moss to the ball.

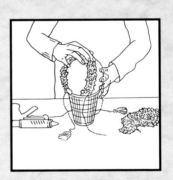

5

6

Fill each section of the ball between the strips of moss with rose heads by pushing the stems into the oasis. Start by making a triangular shape bordering the moss, and then fill this in. If the stem breaks, use a fine wire and gently insert it up through the rosebud. Make a hook on the end that has poked through and pull it carefully back through the middle of the rose. Re-tie the shorter cord into a knot and the tasselled cord into a bow. Decorate the top with a piece of artificial holly.

CHRISTMAS CRACKERS
STEP BY STEP

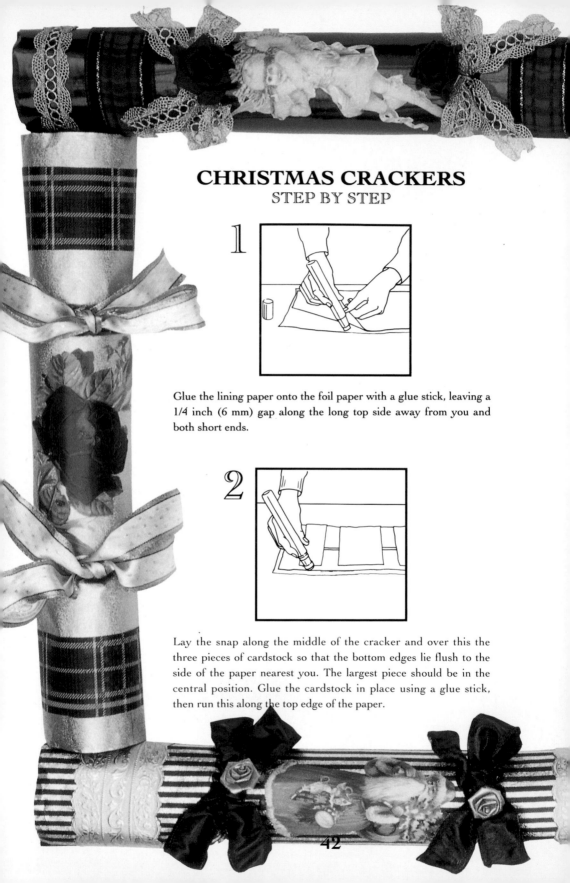

1

Glue the lining paper onto the foil paper with a glue stick, leaving a 1/4 inch (6 mm) gap along the long top side away from you and both short ends.

2

Lay the snap along the middle of the cracker and over this the three pieces of cardstock so that the bottom edges lie flush to the side of the paper nearest you. The largest piece should be in the central position. Glue the cardstock in place using a glue stick, then run this along the top edge of the paper.

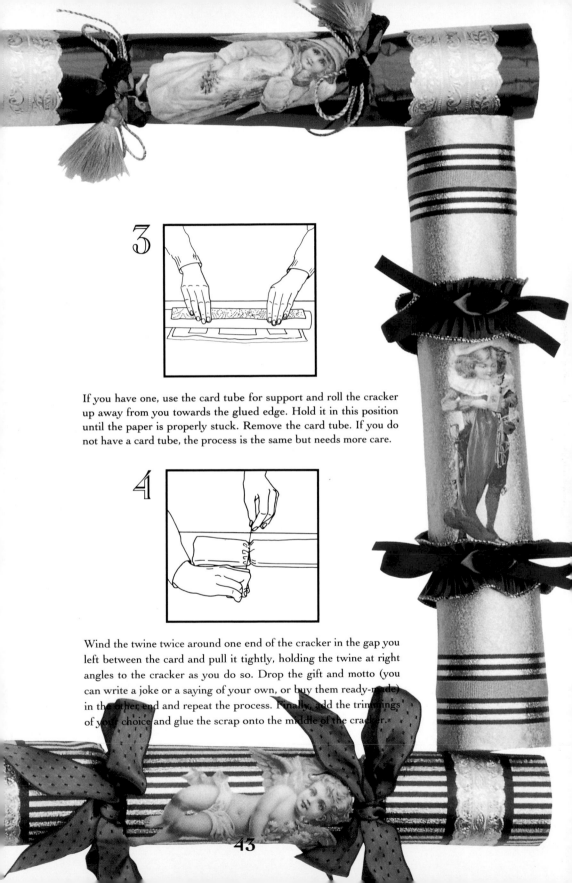

If you have one, use the card tube for support and roll the cracker up away from you towards the glued edge. Hold it in this position until the paper is properly stuck. Remove the card tube. If you do not have a card tube, the process is the same but needs more care.

Wind the twine twice around one end of the cracker in the gap you left between the card and pull it tightly, holding the twine at right angles to the cracker as you do so. Drop the gift and motto (you can write a joke or a saying of your own, or buy them ready-made) in the other end and repeat the process. Finally, add the trimmings of your choice and glue the scrap onto the middle of the cracker.

NEW YEAR'S EVE WASSAIL OR PUNCHBOWL

Historical Perspective :
CHARITY AND WASSAIL
- BOXING DAY

Even in the workhouses, Christmas was celebrated with special food. In *A Christmas Carol*, Scrooge's transformation from vile miser to decent human being is marked by his act of charity to the poor Cratchit family, and Dickens calls on his readers to give to those less fortunate than themselves. Such charitable acts took place on St Stephen's Day or Boxing Day, so called because of the boxes set aside in the churches for charitable donations of food and gifts. Boxing Day had became a public holiday in England by the 1870s.

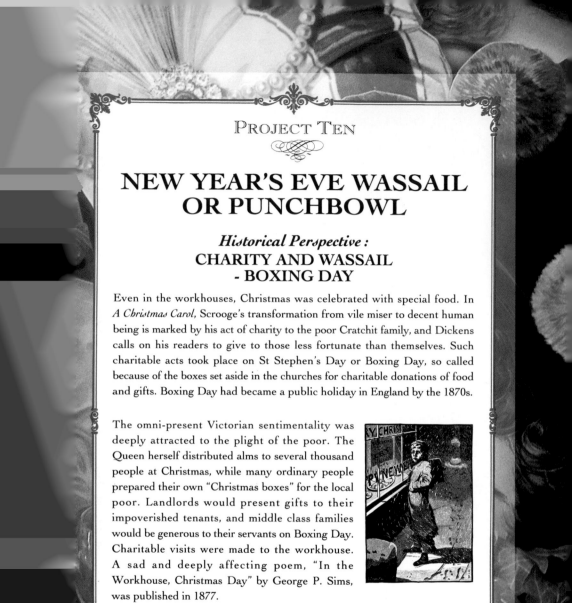

The omni-present Victorian sentimentality was deeply attracted to the plight of the poor. The Queen herself distributed alms to several thousand people at Christmas, while many ordinary people prepared their own "Christmas boxes" for the local poor. Landlords would present gifts to their impoverished tenants, and middle class families would be generous to their servants on Boxing Day. Charitable visits were made to the workhouse. A sad and deeply affecting poem, "In the Workhouse, Christmas Day" by George P. Sims, was published in 1877.

PANTOMIME

The "panto" season traditionally started on Boxing Day as a treat for richer families. Poor people walked the streets wearing boards to advertise them. *Puss in Boots, Cinderella, Babes in the Wood, Jack in the Beanstalk,* and *Aladdin* were all popular and have remained so, but there were others which have sadly not survived the Victorian period, such as *The Ogre of Rat's Castle.* Whatever the story, the sets and costumes were lavish and the melodrama electric.

You Will Need

Large glass bowl
Scraps from sheets 97 & 98
Gold leaf adhesive
8 –10 sheets of gold-colored leafing or foiling
Soft synthetic brush for applying gold leaf adhesive
Soft brush for tamping leaf
Photocopies of Wassail
  song in this book
  (four were used here)
Candle
Dark shellac
Acrylic varnish

NEW YEAR'S EVE

Another tradition was a party on New Year's Eve, to mark the passing of the old year and the start of the new. The wassail, a hot punch made from ale, sherry, brandy or cider, apples, lemons and spices, was a medieval tradition. The brew usually included roasted apples bobbing about on top and was served steaming hot. This warming drink would have been offered along with hot mince pies to carol singers going from house to house or to cold worshippers returning home from midnight mass, or on New Year's Eve at party-time. This project shows you how to make a wassail bowl for your own New Year's Eve celebrations.

The Wassail Bowl.

The word "wassail" is probably based on "wes heill," the old Saxon term for "Good Health". Wassailing was an ancient way of marking the new year, in which young men would storm around the towns and villages beating drums and home-made instruments. This fearful noise was supposed to frighten off the evil spirits. Sometimes country folk would "wassail" the apple trees in their orchards during Christmas to ensure a good crop in the coming year. In this case, shotguns were fired through the branches to raise the sleeping spirit of the tree and frighten off any lurking demons. Some drops of the wassail punch were poured at the roots of the trees, and a piece of bread soaked in wassail was left in the fork of the tree. Then a toast to the tree would be made by all attending, and everyone would sing the wassail song.

Another New Year custom was that of first-footing, in which a young man would make a ritual entrance immediately after midnight, to wish everyone inside the house a happy New Year.

Victorian Christmas celebrations continued until Twelfth Night, on January 6th, which marked the Feast of the Epiphany, when the Three Wise Men were guided by the star to Bethlehem.

In 19th century France people celebrated Twelfth Night as a special occasion in its own right, with its own cake, the *Galette des Rois*, which had a golden crown atop a wafery slab of pastry and ground almonds. It contained a bean or little toy king, and whoever found this token in their portion became king of their household for the day.

All over the world, Twelfth Night marked the end of the Christmas festival, and in Victorian times it was the time for resuming everyday life - time to write the formulaic thank-you letters, time to take down the greenery, time to pack up carefully the glass ornaments, and finally to settle down to the business of keeping the New Year resolutions.

WASSAIL BOWL
STEP BY STEP

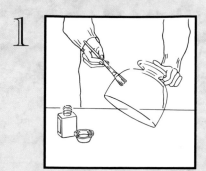

1 Using a soft-haired synthetic brush, paint a thin layer of quick-drying acrylic goldsize onto the outside of the bowl and leave for about twenty minutes until it has become transparent.

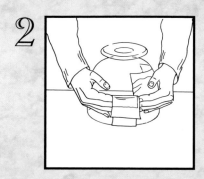

2 Cut each leaf you are using in half. Carefully lay a piece on the bowl and press the back of the transfer paper with your finger tips so that the leaf is transferred onto the goldsize. Continue in this way around the bowl. You may need to cut the leaf into smaller sections to complete the base of the bowl. Use the scraps of leaf remaining on the transfer paper to fill in any gaps you may have.

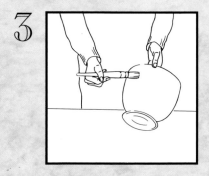

3 Using a soft-haired brush, tamp the leaf down and dust off all the loose pieces. Let the bowl dry out for about a week before applying further decoration.

4 Singe the edges of the wassail photocopies as described in the cookie tin project on page 12 and cut out the fruit scraps. Spray the backs of these with repositionable glue/spray adhesive (remountable) and very carefully arrange them around the bowl. Starting with the photocopies, brush glue onto the back of each piece of paper and stick permanently in place, then stick on the scraps so that they overlap the photocopies in places. Clean off the excess glue with a damp sponge, taking great care not to scratch the delicate surface. Let the bowl dry for two or three hours.

WASSAIL BOWL
STEP BY STEP

5

Paint a coat of dark shellac over the outside of the bowl to age the paper and the leaf. You will need to work quickly with a fairly new varnish brush that is still soft, so as not to leave brush marks. Repeat this process when the first coat feels completely dry if you want to deepen the effect.

6

Give the bowl three coats of satin acrylic varnish, leaving at least two hours between each one, and let it dry another week before using.

TIPS
If you do not feel sufficiently confident to tackle the gold-leafing stage, spray the bowl with gold paint instead. If you would like to try the gold-leafing process, but have no previous experience, experiment on a jam jar first.

RECIPE FOR WASSAIL

2 pints (1.2 litres) ale
1/4 pint (150ml) sherry
1/4 pint (150ml) brandy
1 tablespoon (15ml) sugar
Peel of a lemon cut into strips
Juice of 1 lemon
1/4 teaspoon grated nutmeg

Put all the ingredients into a saucepan and bring to the boil. Simmer for five minutes. Let it cool for a couple of minutes before pouring into the glass bowl. You could also bake some small, firm apples to float in the mixture, if desired.

Here We Come A-Wassailing

Here we come a-was-sail-ing a-mong the leaves so green,

Here we come a-wan-der-ing, so fair to be seen. Love and

joy come to you, And to you your was-sail too, And God bless

you and send you a hap-py New Year, And God send you a

hap-py New Year.